LEMONADE, ANYONE?

No, this isn't an errant page from another self-published how-to book that somehow found its way into **PANCAKE ART**. Lemonade has precious little to do with pancakes, although there must be one or two pancake aficionados out there who enjoy drinking it with their meal. But lemonade is very relevant to a certain shortcoming in this book, which is purely the result of my technological ineptitude.

THIS BOOK HAS NO PAGE NUMBERS!!

Seriously! Whatever I did while writing and formatting the book has resulted in my complete inability to include page numbers without screwing up the book's 6x9 template. I have tried everything I can think of to cure the problem, which clearly must not be enough. So I was faced with one of two options: (A) abandon the book (thus depriving future generations of the fun involved in being a pancake artist or the beneficiary of the artwork), or (B) turn lemons into lemonade. I'm quite certain it's clear which option I chose (even to those of you who really do like drinking lemonade with your pancakes), which has created wonderfully unanticipated opportunities to make owning or gifting this book an even funner family affair. (OK, funner is not a word, but read on and you'll see why it works perfectly here.)

I believe I have invented a whole new facet of self-publication, and a new word to describe it: self-pagination. It really is quite simple. You, the proud owner of this book, get to insert the page numbers by hand! What fun, and by doing so you will get a quick overview of what **PANCAKE ART** is all about.

But what if you bought the book for your children to give the other parent as a gift? Here's where the funner part comes in. Have the youngsters insert the page numbers themselves and encourage them to be creative which, after all, is the main focus of this book. (For example, with any number that ends in 0, let the 0 become the sun). How many books do you have where the kids can personalize it this way before giving it to their mom or dad? After the word gets out about self-pagination, I'm sure there will be plenty more. Aren't you glad this isn't a 300-page romance novel?

For uniformity, I suggest starting with the number 1 on the first page of the Introduction. By doing so, you should end with the number 44 on the last page. But really, who cares? Let the funner begin any way you or the kids decide.

Lemonade, anyone?

INTRODUCTION

Sunday is brunch day for everyone at my house. That includes my wife, daughter and mother-in-law. Brunch usually consists of juice, turken (my daughter's a semi-vegetarian, so we don't have bacon), and pancakes. It's been that way from the time my daughter could eat solid food, and I imagine it will always be that way since she shows no current signs of losing interest in solid food.

One could say we "sit down" to brunch, but that's not literally true. My wife fixes the turken while I mix the pancake batter. When the turken's done, one of us calls our daughter, and the three of us devour the turken standing up, usually around the center island. Then I scrape the griddle, pushing grease and bits of turken into the gutter around the outer edge. Since there isn't enough room on the griddle to make pancakes for everyone at the same time, I prepare each person's meal individually. That means I'm always standing while the others are sitting and enjoying the fruits of my labor.

I always serve my wife and mother-in-law first, but not necessarily in that order. This is done at the request of my daughter. She thinks the first batch of pancakes gets contaminated by the residual grease and turken bits on the griddle, so better to let her mother or grandmother die of such toxins. (It's sort of like the theory behind kings using tasters in the good ole days.) By the time I get to her pancakes, all is right in the culinary world.

The adults always get the "same old-same old" 3 round pancakes of approximately the same size. No big deal there. Simple and fast, but totally lacking in creativity. When it comes to making my daughter's pancakes, however, the artist in me comes alive.

Becoming a pancake artist "par excellence" began after our first trip to Disneyland. We had breakfast one morning at Goofy's Kitchen, where the kids could get incredibly detailed waffles in the shape of Mickey Mouse, which were a great hit with the youngsters. When we returned home, I used the next Sunday brunch to launch my career as a pancake artist by becoming a Goofy chef.

Well, not exactly. My first attempt at creating Mickey Mouse pancakes could only be described as boringly simplistic: one large circle for the head, and two smaller circles for the ears. My audience was duly appreciative, mixing their oohs and aahs with comments like "You've really got talent" and "Yes, we can tell what it is". All in all, however, I'd say it was an inauspicious debut.

But I was hooked by the praise, and like any compliment-seeking artist, I knew I had to create additional masterpieces in order to continue wowing the troops. So I decided on a strategy that was to set the course for my future endeavors. Instead of trying to improve upon my Mickey Mouse design (which, by the audience response from the week before, seemed beyond improvement), I was determined to create new designs, starting with other Disney characters. Hopefully this admission won't subject me to past or future royalty payments to the Mouse House.

My next masterpiece was Pluto (Fig. I.1), and then Goofy (Fig. I.2). The only real way to tell the two apart at this stage was the rudimentary hat I made for Goofy, but my daughter had no trouble identifying the two. (The fact that we had recently been to Disneyland was probably a major factor in her ability to recognize the characters.) I could create these early designs with a big cooking spoon, but I was frustrated by the lack of detail. So inspiration struck, and I began using a turkey (not turken) baster in addition to the spoon. This allowed me to form outlines for my designs, which I'd fill in with the spoon, or a small measuring cup with a handle. Once my artistic spirit was freed from the boundaries presented by the spoon alone, I could soar to new heights of pancake artistry.

But discovering and refining a new talent takes time, patience and ingenuity. So I started with simple shapes, such as a butterfly, which I'll get to later. Then I looked for inspiration in the things around us, such as our dog. When the holidays came, I did thematic designs. If my daughter was involved in an activity, such as playing the piano or riding horses, I'd use that as a source for new ideas. (Later in the book I'll tell you how to create a grand piano with black and white keys.) The possibilities are only limited by your imagination.

As my skill and confidence increased, so did my fame and reputation. I began to create designer pancakes for my daughter's friends that slept over, and for families that visited us. The word spread, and now I'm writing this book to share what I know, and how I do it, with the rest of the world.

Before I get started with the how-to stuff, let me give you one very important suggestion. Never let people see your creation until it's done and assembled. Then watch everyone's response when you present it to the intended diner, and ask him or her to guess what it is. There will be smiles aplenty, and you'll have a great sense of satisfaction at having stolen the show.

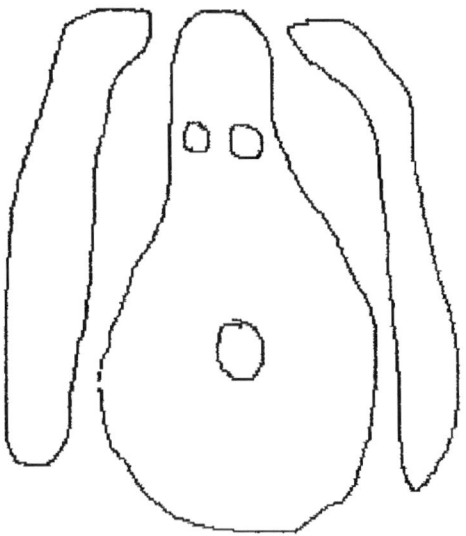

Fig. 1.1 Pluto (The kids will get it, with a clue or two from you.)

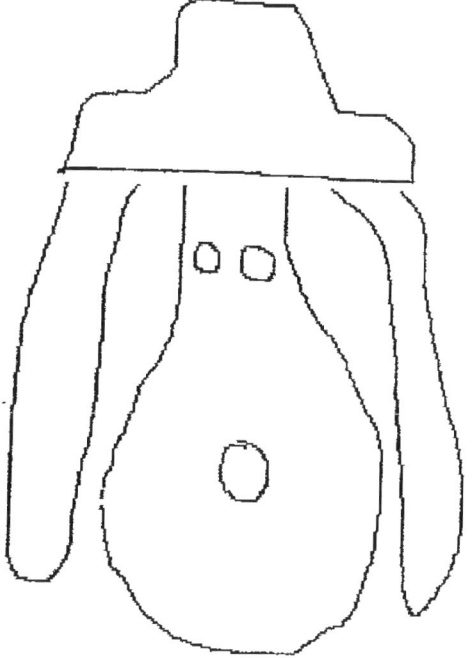

Fig. 1.2 Goofy (Pluto with a hat. Trust me on this one. The kids will get it, with a clue or two from you.)

CHAPTER 1

TOOLS OF THE TRADE

Buying this book proves that you want to put your enthusiasm and imagination to work. If you bought this book as a gift, it merely proves that you want to put someone else's enthusiasm and imagination to work. (Either way, I appreciate the fact that you bought the book.) But you're going to need other tools of the trade to get started on your career as a pancake artist.

At the risk of stating the obvious, it would be hard to become a pancake artist without pancake batter. So be sure you have some handy whenever you decide to take the plunge. I know there may be some purists out there who would prefer to make the batter from scratch, but I for one have never found scratch in the grocery store. The next best thing is ready-made pancake mix. Whatever mix you use, don't forget to buy eggs, milk and oil when you're at the store. And if you want to avoid having egg on your face when you've finished your first masterpiece, be sure to buy butter and pancake syrup, too.

The consistency of the batter is critical, as you'll learn in Chapter 2. So have a whisk on hand to mix the batter and the requisite ingredients.

You'll also need a griddle, which should be the rectangular kind that covers two burners on your stove. (Otherwise, brunch could run into dinner if you're cooking for a large group.) I use a cast aluminum griddle as opposed to a cast iron one, since it's much easier to clean, but either will do just fine.

You can't be a pancake artist without a spatula or pancake turner. It should be metal, and as wide as possible with a beveled front edge. Some of your creations will undoubtedly be large, and it's easier to flip them if you have a wide, beveled spatula. I've tried using a plastic spatula, but over time it tends to develop a slight downward bend at the front edge. This makes it increasingly difficult to get under the pancakes when it comes time to flip them, and has resulted in the ruination of far too many potential masterpieces of mine. To put this in perspective, can you imagine Rembrandt painting with a brush that didn't lay flat against the canvas? (More about him later.)

You must also have a large cooking spoon handy, or a small dipper. I started out using the spoon, but I changed to a plastic measuring cup (1/4 cup in size) with a long side handle and a spout. It gives me much more control over where I pour the batter, and how much I pour out.

But the most important tool of all is a turkey baster, preferably one with a long tube and a narrow tip. This is how you create recognizable designs with amazing details. If you don't have one, don't announce the debut of your career as a pancake artist. Without a baster, you'll be forever doomed to using three circular pancakes to create Mickey Mouse. I know. I've been there.

And finally, keep a salad fork nearby. Salads have nothing to do with pancakes, but the fork will enable you to flip small pieces of your creation much more easily than the spatula.

CHAPTER 2

GETTING STARTED

I'm assuming that you now have all of the necessary tools, you've put your apron on, and you're ready to get started. It's important to keep in mind that the order in which you do things from this point forward, as opposed to the order in which you feed your guests, will have a lot to do with your ultimate success. So I'd read this chapter first before you begin doing anything. You may look a little silly standing around the kitchen with a book in your hand, but trust me, it's worth the embarrassment.

The first thing to do is start the griddle heating. Why, you ask? Because getting the griddle to the right temperature takes longer than just about anything else you have to do. And if you think you look silly walking around the kitchen in an apron reading a book, just wait for people's reactions when you're waiting around for the griddle to warm up. Use a medium setting so the griddle doesn't flash burn the first batter that hits it.

This would also be a great time to have someone else heat up the syrup and set the table. Why, you ask again? Because once your masterpiece comes off the griddle, it will begin to cool rapidly. If people are running around trying to do all of these things right then, I guarantee you the food, its reception and your mood will get very chilly.

While the griddle is heating, mix up the pancake batter. Whatever you've heard about the proper consistency for batter, forget it. We're talking about art here, and art can't be achieved without using the turkey baster, and the baster is useless if the batter can't get in and out of it. So the batter has to be smooth, creamy and completely lump-free. (Think yogurt.) The best way to achieve this result is to mix the ingredients with a whisk until you get the right consistency.

Now you need to test the griddle to see if it's hot enough to cook on. There are two ways to do this. Most people will sprinkle a little water on the griddle, and declare it ready if the water bubbles up and rolls around the surface. Should you choose to test the griddle this way, keep in mind that you're missing a great opportunity to soften up your audience before the show begins.

So here's what a maestro of pancake art should really do. Use the baster and put little pancakes, about the size of a silver dollar, in the middle of the griddle and at both ends. There should be as many silver-dollar pancakes as there are guests, since each guest will get one when they're cooked. (I call them "testers", but my family calls them "tasters".) You've now got the audience eating out of the palm of your hand, or to be more accurate, out of the palms of their hands. What could be better? With one deft move you know that both the griddle and the guests are ready to go.

As soon as you start heating the griddle you should start thinking about what you're going to create, and how you're going to do it. Advance planning is vital, because once you touch batter to griddle, everything happens quickly. There is no time to waste. The batter will cook with or without your creative juices flowing. Any hesitation can bring new meaning to the phrase "crash and burn". Since I'm fond of using analogies to put things into perspective, this is exactly like Chinese wok cooking. It may take a while to plan the meal and prepare all of the ingredients, but once you start throwing them into the wok, everything cooks at warp speed. So stay focused.

Bear in mind that the different pieces of your masterpiece may cook at different speeds, depending on the size of the piece and its location on the griddle. Generally speaking, the smaller, thinner pieces cook more quickly. So you might want to put them on a bit later, or towards the outer edge of the griddle, where batter tends to cook more slowly.

A piece is ready to flip when small craters appear all over it and the edges are slightly firm. You should also lift up a small outer section of the piece to see what color it is underneath. It should be somewhere between golden brown and dark tan. Once you flip a piece over, never flip it again. If it wasn't ready to flip, throw it away and start again.

Here are a few other important points to remember as you move from this stage to the next:

1. Make one masterpiece at a time.
2. Visualize it well ahead of time. If, however, your left brain has never functioned properly, or you don't do well under pressure, don't hesitate to use props or visual aids.
3. Make your masterpiece in parts or sections whenever possible. It's easier to flip smaller pieces, and assembling the design on a plate is definitely a big part of the fun for the artist.
4. Be sure the intended recipient is nearby, but do not let him/her see your creation before it's assembled.
5. Try to design a masterpiece that relates to something the recipient likes or does. This shows that you're a caring and insightful artist, which will play well to those assembled for the event.
6. Never lose your sense of humor or sense of adventure. Having fun and exploring new designs is what pancake art is all about.
7. As silly as it may sound now, you'll thank me for this final piece of advice later: keep a camera handy. Some of your masterpieces will be so clever, and so well received, that you'll want to take pictures of them and the people who got them. (One close friend and her husband were so delighted and impressed that she gave me a framed collage of photos taken at our brunch together.)

CHAPTER 3

BE PICASSO, NOT REMBRANDT

Okay, it's time to put theory into practice. And practice is what it's going to take to get really good at this. But don't be timid about plying your craft. No matter how your first few masterpieces turn out, the audience will love and admire you. Just remember one thing at this point in your budding career as a pancake artist: be Picasso, not Rembrandt.

What I mean by that pithy analogy is very simple, and springs from the very nature of pancake batter itself. Rembrandt, as you may recall, was a master of detail. Everything he painted looked exactly like the real thing. Picasso, on the other hand, was a minimalist. He could draw the human body using just a few lines and curves. And so it should be with pancake artists. For no matter how hard we might try to control it, pancake batter has a mind of its own. We can't achieve precise detail when working with it, so we must strive instead to create simple, generic shapes that represent what we are designing.

Striving to become a Picasso of pancake art has many benefits. It keeps the aspiring pancake artist from going nuts, since realism is not a goal. It also keeps the expectations of the audience to a minimum, which means that they'll undoubtedly think whatever you create is fabulous, even if they haven't got a clue what it is.

If, however, you feel overwhelmed by the thought of trying to design actual objects no matter what famous painter you might want to emulate, then you should try what I have dubbed the "Concentration" approach. Anyone my age will certainly remember the game show Concentration, where contestants had to decipher puzzles that used letters, numbers and pictures to represent words and phrases.

Let me explain how this works. Suppose one of your brunch guests is an optometrist, but you're convinced that it's way beyond your capabilities to design a pair of glasses. So you turn to the Concentration approach, and the phrase "an eye for an eye" hits you like a lightning bolt. You make two "N"s, one "4" and two eyes, which are about the easiest objects to draw with a baster. (An even simpler approach would be to make two "I"s, but that would be nothing more than an admission to your audience that you haven't got a left brain.) Then you put one N and an eye at the top of the plate, the 4 in the middle, and the other N and eye at the bottom. Voila! Another masterpiece.

Once your skills as a pancake artist have developed, you can have all sorts of fun creating Concentration masterpieces. I hit my stride the morning after my wife and I had participated in a friendly late-night poker game with two visiting couples. The other women were a mother and daughter, who co-owned a temp employment agency. Since the mother had cleaned everyone out of their milk money, I wanted to do something poker related. Inspiration struck, and I designed a "royal flush" for her, which was a crown sitting on top of a side view of a toilet (Fig. 3.1). She and the others got it right away, and howled with laughter. I wish I had a photo of that one.

For her daughter, I designed a fairly elaborate pancake woman (Fig. 3.2), and presented it to her as the "ultimate temp". (More about how to design humans in a later chapter.) This one took a while for everyone to figure out, and I had to give them more than one clue. But in the end it received the same enthusiastic response.

These two designs were the ultimate combination of Picasso and Concentration for me. You, too, will reach this level of creativity as you progress in your career as a pancake artist. Fear not.

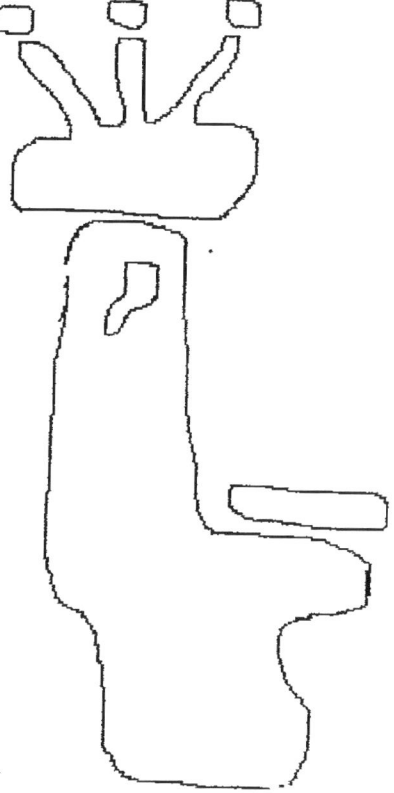

Fig. 3.1 Royal Flush (crown on a toilet)

Fig. 3.2 "The Ultimate Temp" (She's just there for breakfast)

CHAPTER 4

K.I.S.S. and Tell

I learned many years ago that the acronym K.I.S.S. stood for "Keep It Simple, Stupid". I strongly advise all aspiring pancake artists to chant this mantra during the early stages of their artistic endeavors. However, avoid burning incense while chanting, since it could affect the flavor of the batter.

Using the K.I.S.S. principle, let's start with a butterfly, which is always a big hit with pre-schoolers. This will also demonstrate several other key points about pancake art.

This design consists of a cigar-shaped body, two wings and two antennae. With the baster, outline the body first in the middle of the griddle, since this will determine the size of your design. (This was going to be Fig. 4.1, but I couldn't fit three images on one page, so it's not there.). Then outline the wings, which you should keep fairly close to the body so that the dimensions are uniform. Finally, do the antennae, which are just lines of batter that curve in opposite directions (Fig. 4.2).

Now, using the dipper, fill in the body and the wings. Don't panic if the batter spills beyond an outline. After you flip everything, and the batter hardens, you can trim away the overflow using the spatula. Be careful not to do this too soon, however, because you don't want gooey batter sticking to the spatula. This would have to be cleaned off immediately, which could throw your timing completely out of whack.

Once all of the pieces are flipped, cooked and trimmed, assemble them on the plate as shown in Fig. 4.2. Give it to your little brunch guest, and I'm certain he or she will have no problem telling you what it is.

That's how K.I.S.S. and Tell works.

You K.I.S.S. -- They Tell.

When you think you're ready to get a little fancy, you can use the baster to create lines within the wings (Fig. 4.3). This is an important point to remember: you can create lots of solid details within an outline with the baster. Just give the details enough time to harden before you fill in the outline, since they will be more noticeable when you flip that piece over.

And when you're beginning to feel really adventurous, you can create multi-colored masterpieces. My first attempt at color came when I designed a rainbow trout for my daughter, who almost landed one the previous day during a fishing trip. Before starting the design, I put small amounts of batter into four separate bowls and added different food coloring to each one. After drawing the outline of a fish with vertical stripes inside it, I filled in each body section with different colored batter. I used regular batter for the fins. Once assembled, it literally became a rainbow trout, although the colors had a bit of a brownish tinge from being cooked in the batter. No matter -- the colors paled by comparison with my daughter's sheer delight at seeing this masterpiece.

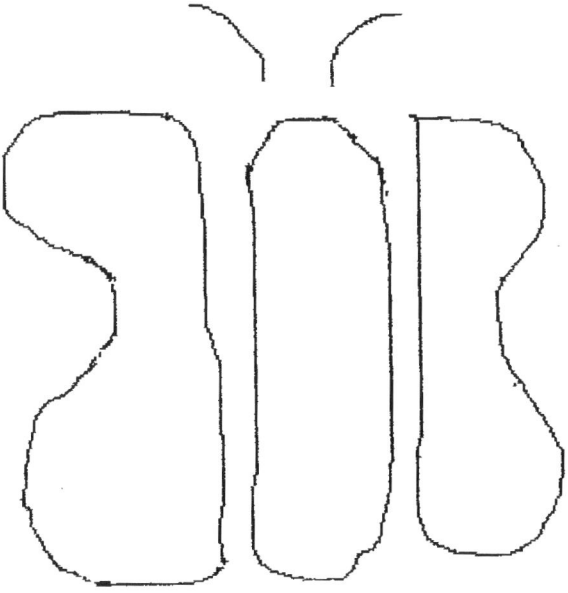

Fig. 4.2 Butterfly with assembled parts

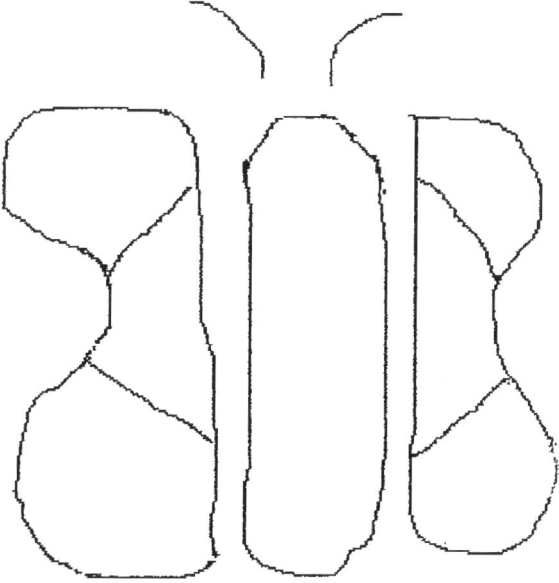

Fig. 4.3 Butterfly with stripes

CHAPTER 5

BODY PARTS

It's inevitable that you'll get into designing animals and people. After all, most of us have a dog, or a cat, or a horse, or a mother, or a father, or a daughter, or a son, or a sister, or a brother, etc., etc., etc. We've always had a dog, and my daughter loves to ride horses. So these animals have figured prominently in the development of my skill as a pancake artist. As for the humans in my life, it took me a while to tackle them as subjects, but once I did, it opened up a new dimension for me to explore. To do this well, you need to feel comfortable designing body parts. Just remember that you're creating works of art for a Sunday brunch crowd, not your late night adult movie friends.

When I got started as a pancake artist, our dog was a mix of terrier and schnauzer, and since we both had the same hair color, we shared a certain cosmic connection. I obviously wanted to make her look good, but I decided it would be impossible to do the whole body. So I focused on doing her head, as if she were looking straight at me.

To do a dog's head (or a cat's head, for that matter), use the dipper to pour out an oval shape. Without stopping the pouring action, go to the middle of the oval and pour some batter straight north, allowing it to taper off at the top. (Fig. 5.1) The overall shape should look a little like a witch's hat with a rounded tip. Now what you need to design are the ears, the eyes, the eyebrows, the nose, the mouth and the whiskers, otherwise known as body parts.

This is when your skill as a pancake artist must come to the fore. You have to customize the parts to look like your pet so that your guests can tell what your creation is. Our dog had short floppy ears (Fig. 5.2), bushy eyebrows that partially covered her eyes (Fig. 5.3), and she often stuck the tip of her tongue just slightly out of her mouth (Fig. 5.4). So that's what I used to make the design look like her. The eyes are small circles, the nose is a triangle and the six whiskers are just straight lines (Fig.5.5). All of this is made with the baster, and you'll need the salad fork to flip some of these pieces. When it came time to assemble everything, I put the eyes on first so that the eyebrows could be placed just slightly on top of them. It wasn't difficult for my daughter to recognize the finished masterpiece (Fig. 5.6), but I can't totally ignore the fact that we only had one dog.

Horses are actually quite easy to do, if you stick with the profile of the body part known as the head. First outline the head (Fig. 5.7) and the mane (Fig. 5.8) with the baster, then make the nostril and eye, which are just dots. Fill in the outlines with the dipper, and assemble when done (Fig. 5.9). If you're a beginner, the end result will make you look far more advanced than you really are.

I feel a confession is in order here. I have never been able to successfully customize a horse's head to look like the one my daughter rides, which caused us both some angst when we once owned two horses. I guess the moral here is don't be Noah or Rembrandt if you want to be totally appreciated as a pancake artist.

As for designing humans, the Picasso principal has to be your guide. A dress is about the best way to depict a woman, and it can come directly down from her head (Fig. 5.10). Arms, legs and feet can be sticks (Fig. 5.11), or you can design them with more detail as your skill improves (Fig. 5.12). Hair for women (Fig. 5.13), and men who are relatively bald (Fig. 5.14), can be added just to be sure the guests know which is which.

Fig. 5.1 Dog's Head

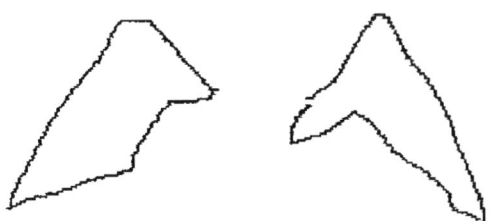

Fig. 5.2 Dog's floppy ears

Fig. 5.3 Dog's bushy eyebrows

Fig. 5.4 Dog's mouth with tongue sticking out

Fig. 5.5 Dog's nose, eyes and whiskers

Fig. 5.6 The finished composition of my Dog's Head

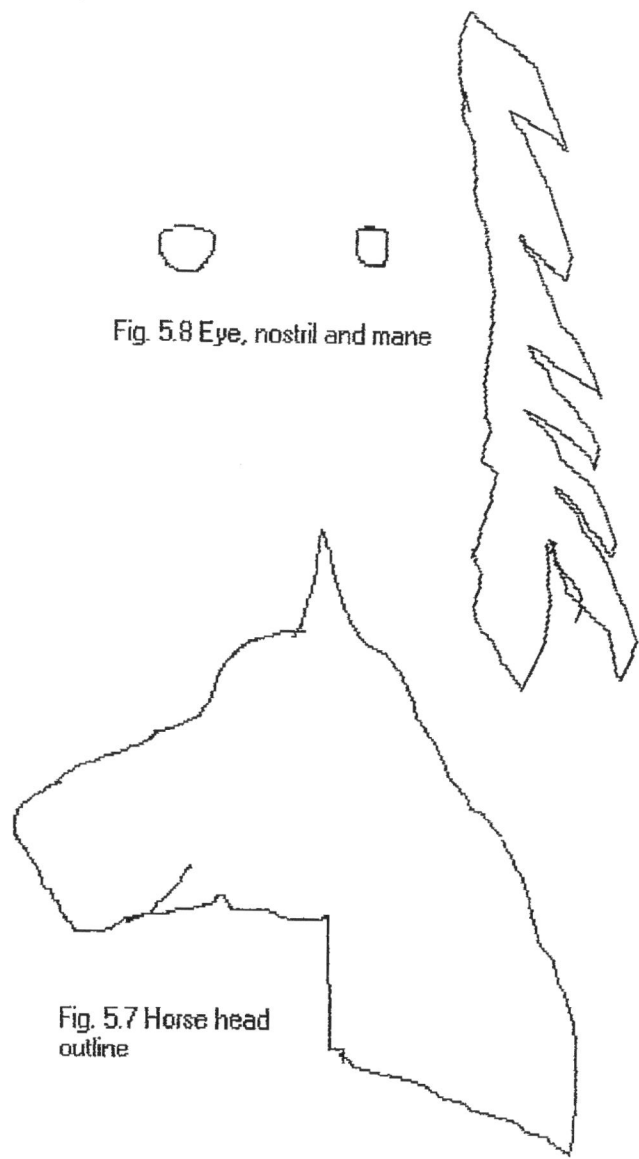

Fig. 5.8 Eye, nostril and mane

Fig. 5.7 Horse head outline

Fig. 5.9 Composite Horse head

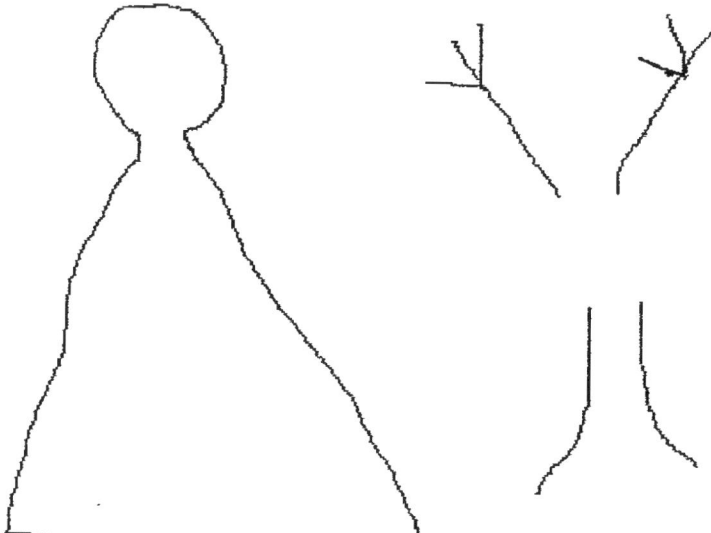

Fig. 5.10 Woman (in dress)

Fig. 5.11 Arms & legs

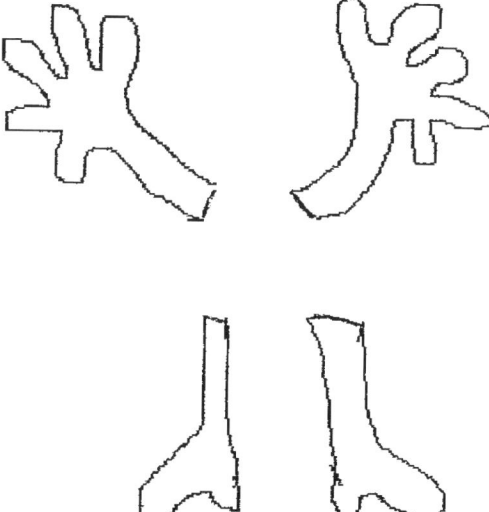

Fig. 5.12 Better defined arms, hands, legs and feet

Fig. 5.13 Hair for women

Fig. 5.14 Hair for men

CHAPTER 6

SOME FINAL (POSSIBLY REPETITIVE) THOUGHTS AND SUGGESTIONS

1. Your artwork has to fit on the plate. So don't scale your artwork to the size of the griddle. Use half the griddle for the main piece, and the rest of the griddle for the additional parts.
2. Don't try to make your artwork all in one piece. That's much too complicated, and it's almost always impossible to flip. Besides, you'll lose the fun of putting the pieces together at the end.
3. Some pieces may turn out to be too big to flip even though you didn't plan it that way. So have a second spatula on hand just in case you need it in an emergency.
4. One side of each piece is always a little darker than the other once it's been flipped and cooked on both sides. This can be used to show contrast if your artwork calls for it. For example, you can create dark and white keys for a piano by simply using different sides of those particular pieces.
5. The design you end up with will be the reverse of the one you started with, since all of the pieces get flipped. This won't matter in most instances, but many numbers and letters have to be done in reverse when first put on the griddle so that they come out the right way once they've been flipped. You'll get the hang of it after awhile, but you should do all numbers and letters in reverse when you're starting out just to be on the safe side. (The illustrations in this book are all done on a pre-flipped basis.)
6. Open spaces can be created within the interior of your artwork. Simply use the baster to outline the space, and then use the dipper to fill in around it. For example, you can create windows for a house by outlining squares, and then pour the batter around them. You can also use this technique to

create the strings on a tennis racquet. Just don't pour any batter inside the outline of the racquet once you've put in the strings.
7. It's inevitable that batter will spill over the outline of your artwork. Don't panic, and don't do anything until you've flipped the piece. Then just before you're ready to take it off the griddle, use the front edge or corner of the spatula to trim away the excess batter.
8. I prefer to separately design all of the additional pieces needed to create the final artwork. This includes eyes, noses, ornaments for a Christmas tree, etc. But you can do this within the body of the main piece by placing them inside the outline and letting them cook in place for 10-15 seconds before you fill in the rest of the outline with batter. They will stand out when you flip the entire piece, but it won't be as impressive (or as gratifying) as assembling separate pieces at the end.
9. Always have a camera handy, and photograph each completed piece of artwork. It's even more fun to get a picture of the recipient holding up the plate, since that way the photo is sure to include a big smile.
10. BE CREATIVE, BE WHIMSICAL, AND HAVE FUN!

CHAPTER 7

INSPIRATION

For those of you who may have difficulty coming up with ideas for your artwork, here are just a few to get you going. But ideas can come from anywhere. There might be something your guest is doing, has done, likes, dislikes, read, saw, won, lost, wears, says, etc. Whenever possible, create something that has relevance to him or her. It will get the most wonderful response.

PROFESSIONS

Lawyer	Scales of Justice, Gavel
Doctor	Stethoscope, Syringe with needle
Realtor	House with windows, door and chimney
Pilot	Plane

SPORTS/HOBBIES/GAMES

Roller blading	Roller blade skate (Fig. A.1)
Ice Skating	Skate (Fig. A.2)
Basketball	Sneaker, Ball with lines
Tennis	Racket, Net
Ping Pong	Paddle, Net

Riding	Horse head (Fig. 5.9), Saddle, Tall boot
Poker	Any card, Royal flush (Fig. 3.1)
Winner	Blue Ribbon (perhaps in color)
Golf	Club, Shoe with spikes, Bag with clubs
Football	Ball, Helmet
Baseball	Bat, Ball with lines
Skiing	Person on skis (Fig. A.3)
Boating	Life jacket (Fig. A.4), Sailboat
Canoeing	Canoe, Paddle, Canoe with paddle
Fishing	Rod and reel
Bowling	Ball with holes, Pins
Pool	8 ball, Rack with 15 balls and a cue
Music	Grand piano with black and white keys (Fig. A.5), Notes on grid, Saxophone, Guitar, Flute

Award   Blue ribbon (using blue-
                               dyed batter)

ANIMALS, INSECTS, FLOWERS

Horse   Head with mane
                               (Fig. 5.9)

Dog   Head (Fig. 5.6),
                               Pluto (Fig. I.1),
                               Goofy (Fig. I.2)

Butterfly   (Fig. 4.2)

Turtle   (Fig. A.6)

Turkey   (Fig. A.7)

Rabbit   (Fig. A.8)

Dolphin

Whale

Dragonfly

Bird

Hummingbird

Elephant

Tulip

Daisy

HOLIDAYS/CELEBRATIONS

Christmas	Santa, Santa's hat, Rudolph (Fig. A.9), Frosty (Fig. A.10), Tree with ornaments (Fig. A.11), Sleigh, Stocking, Ornaments, Angel, Wreath with a bow, Presents with ribbons
Chanukah	Star of David, Minora
New Year's Eve	Year in numbers, Party hat, Blower
Easter	Bunny (Fig. A.8), Basket, Decorated egg
Fourth of July	Flag, Firecracker
Halloween	Carved pumpkin Witch's Hat, Broom, Ghost, Cat, Skeleton
Thanksgiving	Turkey (Fig. A.7), Pilgrim's hat with buckle
Birthday	Cake, Cake with Candles

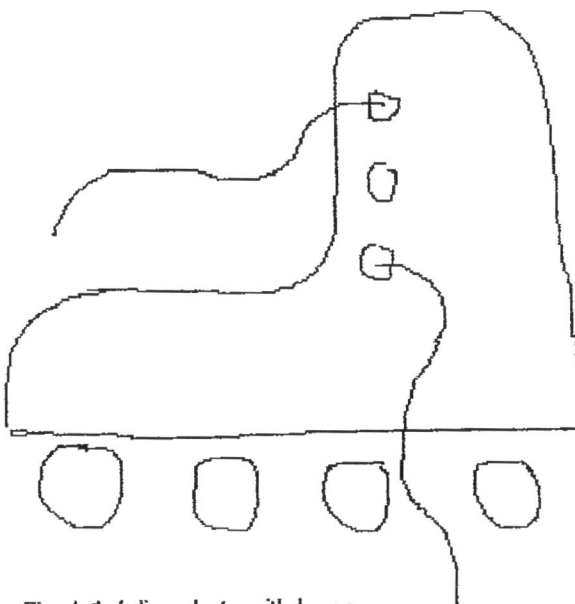

Fig. A.1 Inline skate with laces

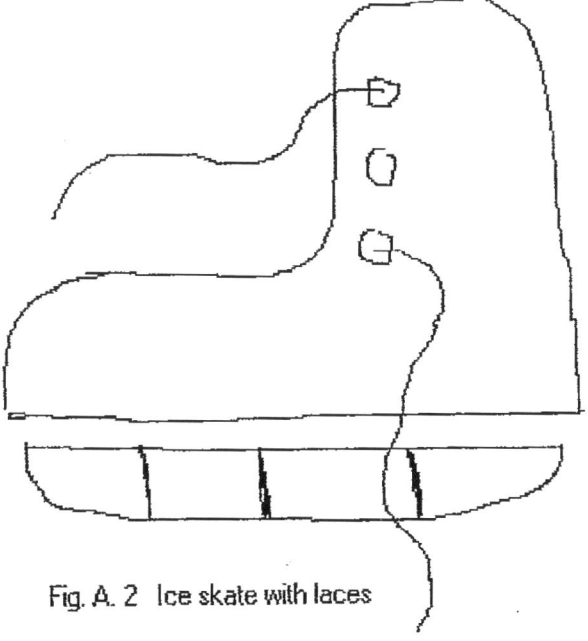

Fig. A. 2 Ice skate with laces

With no wheels or blade, this can be a sports sneaker for an athlete.

Fig. A.3 "Save Yourselves!" (Woman out of control on skis)

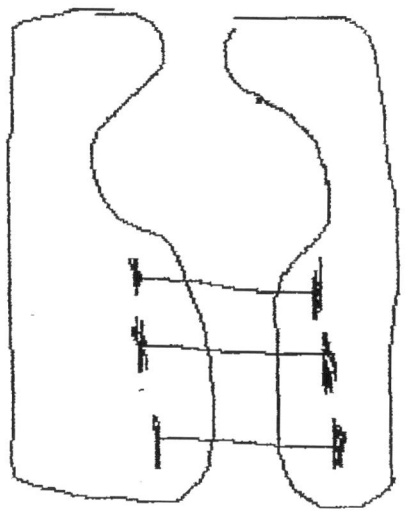

Fig. A.4 Life vest

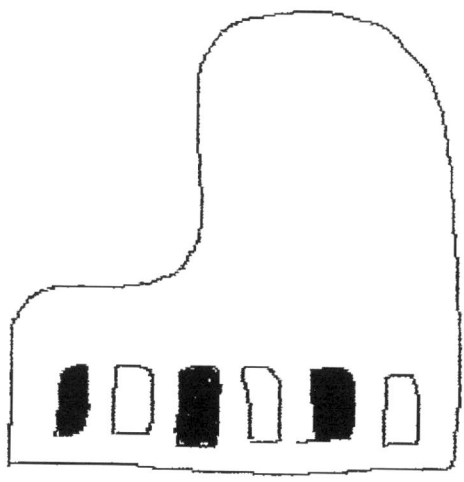

Fig. A.5 Grand Piano (with black and white keys)

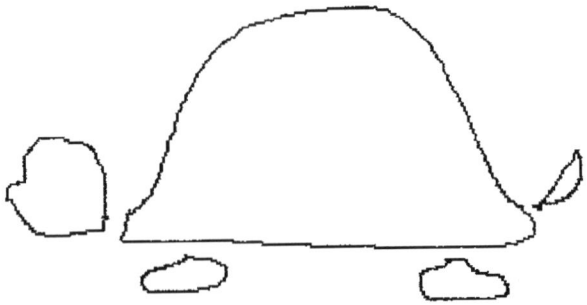

Fig. A.6 Turtle (with or without feet)

Fig. A.7 Turkey

Fig. A.8 Rabbit/Bunny (with the tail on, the view is from behind. If you remove the tail and add eyes, the view is from the front. Only the real Picasso could have it both ways.

Fig. A.9 Rudolph (Use red M&Ms or Life Saver for nose, and brown M&Ms for eyes. Mouth is optional.)

Dipper can be used to create the head by starting with a round pancake and then drawing the batter north as you finish pouring.

Fig. A.10 Frosty/Snowman with hat (can be decorated with M&Ms)

Fig. A.11 Christmas Tree (can be decorated with M&Ms)

CHAPTER 8

OUR LITTLE SECRET

I'll share one final insider secret with you before you get started on your first work of art. You may have noticed that the designations for the illustrations in Chapter 7 begin with an "A" instead of a "7". That's because the chapter was originally the Appendix, and it was simply easier just to leave the designation alone when I changed the heading. But like any good whodunit novel (which this book obviously is not), don't give away the ending. Let readers of all ages discover for themselves the secret and fun of **PANCAKE ART**!

EPILOGUE

There you have it. Everything you need to know to become a pancake artist, the talk of the town and the envy of every family that doesn't have such a culinary genius in residence.

Obviously, I haven't thought of every possible design that can be created with pancake batter, which is where you come in. I plan to do another book, so please take as many photos as possible, and send them to me, along with any suggestions for improving upon my techniques. I'll give you full credit for anything I use and an autographed copy of the book when it comes out, but no money. Your true reward will be the satisfaction you'll get from knowing you're a world-renowned pancake artist, admired by family and friends everywhere.

Photos and suggestions can be sent to me at the following address:

Barr Potter
Tripod Entertainment, Inc.
17939 Chatsworth St. #364
Granada Hills, CA 91344
bb_potter@live.com

Made in the USA
Middletown, DE
28 July 2018